T0209985

Copyright © 2020 Dége.

All rights reserved. No part of this book may be used or reproduced by
any means, graphic, electronic, or mechanical, including photocopying,
recording, taping or by any information storage retrieval system
without the written permission of the author except in the case
of brief quotations embodied in critical articles and reviews.

Balboa Press books may be ordered through booksellers or by contacting:

Balboa Press
A Division of Hay House
1663 Liberty Drive
Bloomington, IN 47403
www.balboapress.com
1 (877) 407-4847

Because of the dynamic nature of the Internet, any web addresses or
links contained in this book may have changed since publication and
may no longer be valid. The views expressed in this work are solely those
of the author and do not necessarily reflect the views of the publisher,
and the publisher hereby disclaims any responsibility for them.

The author of this book does not dispense medical advice or prescribe
the use of any technique as a form of treatment for physical, emotional,
or medical problems without the advice of a physician, either directly
or indirectly. The intent of the author is only to offer information
of a general nature to help you in your quest for emotional and
spiritual well-being. In the event you use any of the information in
this book for yourself, which is your constitutional right, the author
and the publisher assume no responsibility for your actions.

Any people depicted in stock imagery provided by Getty Images are
models, and such images are being used for illustrative purposes only.
Certain stock imagery © Getty Images.

Print information available on the last page.

ISBN: 978-1-9822-4228-2 (sc)
ISBN: 978-1-9822-4227-5 (e)

Balboa Press rev. date: 01/28/2020

CONTENTS

Part I Trust to Ground Yourself

Part II *Love Yourself to Want and Create*

Part III *You are Enough to Have the Wisdom and Power to Act*

Part IV Peace to Love and Heal

Part V Voice to Motivate and Speak

Part VI Intuition to See and to be Aware

Part VII Resilience to Know and to Learn

DEDICATION

To Cortney Ritchie-Davis who has been my lifelong friend and was there when I started putting pen to paper. Thank you to my beta readers and spell checkers Allison Reed, Kristen Davis and Elizabeth Jasmund. Most of all my PR editor and friend Tamra Artelia Martin, her patience and guidance made all of this possible.

PREFACE

I dreamed of this book for young women who think they are alone and that what they feel is not felt by others. We all struggle, and we all feel things that we think we are alone in experiencing. The universe has a bigger plan than you can see when you are searching for your own identity. I struggled as a teen growing up without a father and with an alcoholic mother, not having the love and support close to me, which, at the time, I felt that I so deeply needed.

My journey sometimes led me to bad choices and temptation by others. I searched throughout my teens for answers. I looked to my peers for love that I thought I needed to feel complete. Every obstacle and challenge I had growing up gave me the opportunity to grow and learn from those experiences, which fall into these pages of poetry.

INTRODUCTION

The struggle of growing into a young woman is different for everyone. We all have a story. We all grow in our own time. Don't let your story end before you have a chance to see where it can go and who you can become.

Clocks of human goals
Restricted by minutes to grow
My Spirit
My Soul
Endless time of clocks
Eternity to see where I have been
And where I will go.

Lessons for today
For later time is just to heal
My Spirit
My Soul
In this human body
I chose to be where I have been today
And where I will go.

Trust

to

Ground

Yourself

One, Three, Seven

You amaze me
disappoint me
and confuse me
by never telling me the truth,
but who am I,
not to read and look deep into
what you have written.

If one is to look
into things around them
who is right,
who becomes wrong
if one story can be told
more ways than you
and I can ever write.

It took one illusion for me
to look at you with love.
It took no words for me to doubt
every letter you type with your hands
as a guide to what your thoughts craved.

One day became three,
than seven, turned into thirty days
and now never.

Have you saved everything I wrote?
Word for word I have every syllable
you have written.
Among my readings,
I reread them,
one last time before I said good-bye.

Cause this is the seventh day,
this is how two people say bye,
when they might have never been introduced
as two souls.
as two that one thought was real.

One day became three,
than seven, turned into thirty days
and now never.

The Labyrinth

Like a stone in front of my feet, it lays
Nothing around me seems to go my way
While standing alone here, words were said to me
How hurt gets heavier, blind it made me see
Sitting alone and thinking, wondering how I
Can start a journey by first saying good-bye

I have focused and now come to comprehend
I must have traveled and taken a wrong bend
The leaves are beginning to fall from the wind
Though I have so many messages to send
Standing before me a tall thick patch of trees
Somehow, all around me I can feel them breathe

They are soaking up the moisture in my pores
I turn back, sacrificing myself for more
Look around to find what's on the other side
That's where I should have traveled before the lies
The other people I had loved failed to see
My close friends do not understand the real me

Their eyes, them looking down on me without grace
Among this world we hold, I know there's one place
I have lived a million stories to unfold
Feelings of nowhere to go, bodies to hold
I get back to my dreams before I realize
The beauty that's out there, right before my eyes

Silently I hear cries for me in the air
Finally sensing echoes of voices that care
Though the path I chose to travel did bring pain
Unanswered questions, are confused how we blame
My ears are filled with noises of the crashing sounds
Flowing liquids of strength of all kinds around

I stepped out with pieces of my mold
I brace myself for the cries and the cold
I am breaking away from this old pattern
Creating a new life worth a page turn
I stood here alone, the start of a journey
By first saying good-bye to old me

How Can, One Day

Can one lay there in pleasure that
someone other than you gave?
You breathe guilt from unnecessary
feeling of dishonesty.
She understands the want of your warm
flesh wrapped in her hands.
She questions the way you won't stop
to discover passion in her eyes.

One day, one afternoon, a few hours to
take in the belief of who she is.
If a bed was unavailable, a room of
four undecorated white walls
were gone from the sight of your eyes.
Would that help answer the questions she ponders
without words of vocabulary you speak.

Can you lay there in pleasure that
someone else gives you?
Turning words, she speaks into your own thoughts
that you cannot express.
She barriers guilt from all she knows,
friends never seem to be what they are.
She is left with questions of how she understands.
Stop to listen, to know, to trust in her.

Pain

You are there,
but I can't touch you.
I hear your voice
but I can't make out the words.
Why do you do this?
Play games with my mind
and seduce with my heart.
Would you?
Would someone I trusted,
I like you.
Can't you feel the pain too?
Don't you know what I am going through?

Should Have Been You

In all my life
never did I
feel the feelings
of being used.
The one of you
that's right, you.
I still was happy
laughing in tears
now I hate it.
Her the thoughts of you
her thoughts of everyone.
I want it to be me,
you and me.
Why do I do it,
it is being used
yes used,
that's how I feel now.
Now that she answered the phone
when it should have been you.

Resistance

I want to get to know you,
as if you were me and I was her.
The lashes that drip tears when you cry.
Through your soul of your hearts lies.
The lips that kiss the tears away
are of a stranger's heart.
The stranger learns to leave for a while
and watch from a distance.
You can tell you had a feeling of something
you never had the feelings of resistance.
The one of someone caring enough, to give.

I have come to cradle in my arms
one so gentle in warmth,
but a stranger I can't resist.

Disgrace

You disgrace me
You make me
You thrill my body
You have no control

I still have a thought
Of what it would be
If you kiss me
Would I kiss you
If your hand was in mine
Would I hold it
If your body was next to mine
Would I caress it

By now everything you do
Do you actually think
Think a moment I would do the same
No, because you don't think
One kiss, one hand, one touch
It is not me, not mine
The one in bed with you every night
Won't do the same
I won't do the same
That you don't do for me.

I Know

I know that look of shear mystique.
I know that feeling of letting go.
I know those eyes and what I see.
I know the words, strong sound of noise.
I discovered thoughts and desires.
I desperately need to know something
I don't know if you would kiss my lips
With your arms around my ribs
If you know the feeling of the first touch
The first glance
The first inner feeling of wanting.

I know she watches from a distance.
Knowing if I touch you,
Your lips meet mine; I am my thoughts.
That day will happen,
But till then I will be a patient as I can.
As loyal as I can
Respectable as I can.
I can and most of all be a friend.

Tears Can Be

Too soon,
I know, but how could I feel this.
How could we in 3 weeks
Is it an amount of time,
we trust.
Time to grow
Though we must ask questions
That have answers
Be completely honest.
Praise but never lie
Even if it might make the others cry.
Due to the fact tears can be wiped away
Love takes time to heal
The love for you no matter what
Tomorrow is stronger than gravity
Missing you is the saddest things
I would have to endure.
To soon,
I know,
but I feel this way.
Please make sure the truth is always first
Even if a hearts break
Cause tears can be wiped away,
and a life will be saved.
For death due to love is a mistake
from an angel in the heavens.

Ears Like a Rabbit

Like a fairy
With drops of dust glowing behind
I opened the door to see you.
I walked with you hand in hand
to meet the man.
You told me of secrets.
Now you have gone home with me
To every morning we wake to a kiss.
Every night we fall asleep in arms of support,
making me feel the trust and
excitement of you and me.
Making me smile cracks the face,
like a fairy with drops of dust you walk with me
in all the lights of others.

Course Of

I would know how
how to turn my back
on what I know you can be
The how do I turn my back
on what could have been
If my decision is the only one that seems
to change the course of so many lives.

I would know how to turn my back
on what I don't know could happen
One day you could decide to change
You could decide to be that one
that seems to know
and understand me.

Never Broken

I like your smile,
your moves that groove,
your body to another dimension.
The floor around you slides to the beat
the limbs of your body controlling the air.
Intense,
your body stands under you,
hovering the room.
You are simply glancing my way,
the reach of your hand,
pleasing my soul deep into a trace for you.
I like the way you make me smile.
The way you walk your own path,
with no need to follow.
Sounds of you,
remain in my head.
Sweet words you hold
on that one day.
You will share with someone special
that remains on the brain.
That rains with sad loneliness
in a time of need.
Please understand my need of a friend.

To hold me,
make me feel
as if there is a reason I'm here.
You seem to know how,
when to make a smile appear.

Playing the game of life and see who wins.
The one with words that move through my ears,
or the one with a hand that holds
me through the years.
The mistakes I make are forgiven,
as long as trust and honesty
is never broken.

Unexplainable

Who do you trust,
When you are in need.
Who do you ask,
When your heart bleeds.

The loneliest feeling is having no one to hold,
No one to make you feel as if you
are the only one for them.
When the wind blows
you will feel it in your pours.
When you bathe
the water seeps and drains from you
When you eat
it travels throughout parts of you.
When you love someone
the feeling is untraceable though it travels
and spreads throughout the flesh of the body.
Feelings of unexplainable trust.

What if Tomorrow

Death seems so pleasant
when the one person I thought
I could never lie to or hate,
no longer believed in me.
I want to die
wanting to be gone from the lies
everyone made me tell myself.
The need I needed I never felt
I deserve a fairytale romance,
with someone who doesn't judge my past.
I am truly not the person I want to be,
I really have no way to change
with you here.
Everyone expects so much
that I lie to one to give to another
No one really knows what I want,
no one ever asked the simple question.

If you could change your path
where would you be
and with who would you be only with?
My only wish is to be with one person
in one pair of arms
and one person to romance me.

Someone who wants to hold me
or know about my day.
I can't be the person I am anymore
all I do is try to make everyone else happy.
I never gave myself
the things I took from my soul.
My self-respect that I had that were the things
I believe don't seem to come around.

I want a day to pass without tears
that I can't explain.
What if tomorrow, brought that joy,
where would I go, and with whom do I trust?

Jealous

Never did I think I would be jealous,
I thought I could walk away.
You showed me differently by speaking
her name.
Though our relationship never.
It seemed to change after that day
we became just friends
I felt the strong force of losing you
that brought black clouds my way.
I was the only one who needed your love.
You were the only one I wanted to love.
So how come I was sure to leave you.
When I knew I needed you?
I learned of this jealousy,
I now can learn to love and trust myself.

Letting You Go

One more night I feel alone,
the cold penetrates my bones.
You don't have a clue,
that I have seen you.
How could you, just yesterday?
When among my sheets you lain.
You can't even ask me why, I cry,
when you must tell her, all lies.
She thinks she knows you,
but I had all of what was new.
You are not what you say you are,
I have watched you from afar.
You think I want things my way,
not going to go through this other day.
When I cannot sleep or even breathe,
I just want you to leave me be.
How I feel when you're not near,
when I cannot see you, I cry a tear.
I am not to blame,
when you don't think I feel your pain.
You hide and cheat.
I have you seen the range of desire and heat.
Though I don't know if this is how,
it is going to begin to end now.
I don't want to wait till you walk out the door,
because then I might want you more.

Will you be here tomorrow too?
Or is today the last day for you?
These continuous of lies have left me,
and I am not what you want me to be.
Can't you understand who I have become,
when words became few or none.

I can't watch myself bleed,
when you think I am insane.
I am not what you want me to be,
why can't you see?

I don't know what you knew,
but I want you out of my life.
Do you hear and see my strife?

Love Yourself

to

Want and Create

Plain and Simple

Plain and simple
one long day
to run and play
how heavy the load
with the cold
coming closer tonight
and down the path
maybe in my sight
I draw a bath
made from a pond
in the shelter of winter
they will bond
becoming closer
overhead it becomes
what is it
oh, I might see
it seems to be
one flock of bees
to bring the sweet
to see the sky
for it is blue
with white snow
in the summer heat

I feel the beat
of tiny feet
maybe behind
or in front of me.

Plain and simple
I can feel
this is strange
from what I have known
can you see
or are you
blind like me
I feel and
touch and
hear them near.
For you can't tell
me I am not here.

Plain and simple.

Why That Night

Normal is how I felt and looked.
That night I walked
through the doors and in their path.
I could feel their sight
I could feel their eyes.
Deep within me
thinking what I thought,
as I stopped to look around.
Our eyes met, we knew then,
that is where it was, the truth.

Normal clothes, why that night.
She looked in every way right.
Two opposites
though behind the eyes we told a story.
That would last days or two.
Just not that night
not their ideas
why that night
why not tomorrow.

I Will See You

How do you tumble in love?
What brings you to me?
When I am gloomy and in pain
What restrains you
from the words you want to speak
what holds me from loving you
where are you
I keep driving
I cannot find you
are you going to find me
am I in the wrong place
call my name so I can hear you
I am lonely
I need to hear you
It is as if I want you to appear
as if you know I am thinking of you
as if I know what you look like
why have I not found you
have you dreamed of me yet
I thought I saw you in my dreams last night
how long must I be alone
needing and wanting that someone I haven't met
cannot bare this anymore
trying to find home
yet not knowing the direction
how many more years

till I come across the soul
who dreams like dreams I do
how will you hold me
how will you know
I know
I will know by the look in your eyes
the touch of your hand
the kiss of your lips
especially the words you speak
as your arms hold me
when I need you at night
in the warmth of the covers
the words you can't speak
everyday you become closer
I feel the days getting shorter I cannot wait
Tomorrow is another day
night I see you in my dreams.

Letter

I am writing this letter due to our fact
not knowing your face intensifies
the thought of meeting you
it clarifies every word you speak
now knowing
I will listen.
I will write.

My Friend

As you sat with me
I looked up and there I saw
a desire for me
you had in a moment
your touch did make me
know how to say
how to say no
as I teased you
you played me
as I want you
you are my friend
just to love me.

Broken

You sit far from me
you but a distance
your mind is close to me
it is over lapping with my thoughts
even though you sit in another room
I am sitting with you listening to her
thinking with you
don't get me wrong
I still need more to understand
you for the way you smile
walk and dress
turning on my switch
that was broken.

Help Me to Grow

Do I make you think
when there is no need to
do I ignore you in time of need
please bring the unnecessary thoughts
of my mind when I think of you
learn what I speak
speak what I have learned
as we wonder frequently
about in a time of anguish and sorrow
time now I must tell you
what I forgot
what I am about is
not what you think is me,
Help me to grow.

I Saw Myself

I saw myself go under time
as the clouds shifted
and they stepped by stepping
as I drive these widely roads to the end
that is just a beginning of our travels.

Your skin raised to mine
I felt the comfort,
the knowing of peace
we all three remaining as one somehow.

Though we tangled and untangled ourselves,
to find our thoughts thinking the same.
To speak without fear and to reach out
and touch without a hesitation.

Now time to wait we fill the distance
and togetherness of our friendship.
I saw time over me,
as the clouds shifted
and they stepped by stepping
to the next heart beating.

Desired Kiss

do you want to be
when I am the only one
you look upon
do you want to feel
what she wants
or she wants you to feel
do you really feel
if I feel the feeling you felt

I have wanted to kiss you
sensing you holding back
now this time I must say
to our bodies
we want sometime together
we need to change
the way we met
so we can meet
in the craving
a fire
a fix
on giving
that feeling
you don't go
don't we do together
together we touch the sun
skins apart as we were
we might be

this second in time
between my thighs
I feel a fix
I need to get that desired kiss

An Escape

I feel the need to escape,
to walk a small path
short enough so I can still return,
long enough to change
to escape.

How Can We

as the first time again
as if I was new to you
as if you hold me
as if you never touched my heart
as if my eyes were new to you
can we make our love feel
like the first time again
how can we create a thought
create a dream
as the first time again

Old

These walls were our dreams a year in ½ ago.
This new beginning for a confusing century.
How we met, just two souls in need of someone.
Just like them, who would understand,
not demanding who could love,
not hating to control the other.
To lend a hand and softly hold each other
with others or doubt there would ever be another.
I feel you are the last,
the others are temptation you desire.
I will fulfill your fantasies.
I will make your dreams come true,
if I know myself.
Am I the reason your heart beats?
We have had and will go through
tried for many years to come.
The silence rings through the house
as for every fear we hate.
Did we mislead the truth?
Lead me to you.
How can I learn from you?
What can I teach you?
That you will want to learn.
How could our heart beat if we are one?
A smile is all I need,
To bring a cheer to my body for the touch

you will always give back.
This is the beginning,
now the end of a new beginning.
We have become one in the past months.
I am willing to be a stronger hand
that can direct you through thick and thin.
I love you with words that mean a thousand times
more than I can express.
Do you want, what so many say, we have?
In the eyes of others,
we used to be the sparkle of all our kind.
You are everything in a million ways to me.
You are my life.
There is no replacement to me as dear as you,
I can't breathe without your breath.

Believe In

When a day turns into new,
running nights into the path of you.
You make my soul feel,
something I know is real.

Time keeps parting us.
We need not to be in any rush.
I have not forgotten your smile,
It will be in my mind, a while.

The pictures explain it all.
Me and you were what I saw,
Be my friend,
Dreams with me until the end.

Who can remain with me,
through thick and thin it will be.
We will have stories to tell,
that will help our love grow so well.

I will be here to the end,
when you need a friend.
I will be a shoulder to cry on,
Someone to understand the bond.

Don't give up hope in us,
even through the yelling and fuss.
Through thick and thin,
between friends.

Believe in me,
Believe in you,
the world will never be blue.
When I am around you.

lowers

Like a flower that grew.
Before the rain it fell
then the wind
broke all the petals away,
One last time the flower knew,
before its sight became a memory.

Who would have known that the flower cried?
Who would have saw what it had to offer?
Who would have known that the flowers died?
Among a field of weeds, it grew.
Like a flower of new.

Understanding

Buzz,
I can hear
I knew you heard me too.
The sound doesn't go away
merely does it take a break.
It is here to stay within my ears
for as long as I can hear.

Pain,
I can feel
I know you feel it too.
The way the body can't relax
nothing to do but raise a grief
for the hurt within.
Deep inside a passing stranger
that can feel a present soul nearby.

Blur,
Can it be seen through?
I can only hear and feel
for when I speak,
I speak to strangers without faces,
but voices making me feel warm inside.
need to see if the will,
help me understand,
and see what I can't.

You Are Enough
to
Have the
Wisdom and Power
to Act

That Moment

That moment
time had stopped all together for you.
you walked by,
not noticing how I gazed at your body.
Your eyes said everything.
everything I needed to know
to know you felt what I felt.

Still that moment
did not give me enough time.
Time to look you in the eyes
to let you know I feel the same.
How I could not stand to see you
walk out the door
into the crowd of blank faces, you went.
I was blinded by the light,
I scream inside,
so I am not to be heard.
Still I cannot find you.

Before long the crowd disappeared
still, I remain alone.
Loneliness I feel and see all around,
You were in my life for a second,
Made me feel something,
no one else had ever done.

I lust one thing
that is to kiss the lips
that hold your thoughts,
and secrets from the world.

Night and Day

She gazed at me, not even asking why.
She was all the reason for my pain.
I had to learn to let go, say good-bye.
I am surprised she even came.

She never had to kiss me or put her arms in mine.
How could this be, all I asked for was time.
Time to hold her, love her true.
Without people to slander our feelings.
Now that she left, I feel blue
Years it will take for me to heal.
She was the girl I loved true.

Night and day, she is on my mind.
Can't pick up to phone,
it has been disconnected.
Can't drive to her house,
the roads have been ripped out.
Can't send her a letter,
my words are too confusing.

I can't write and make hell of sense.
writing words to myself.
Why doesn't she understand
she is what I desire.
Night and day bewildered.

Commenting

I have done it again
I felt that body
not one I have known to long
just long enough to touch.

Their fingers lying between mine
as a grip was holding tight
there is nothing to replace this
nothing to fill my need.

Committing to each other.
is not something new,
it is something hard to understand.
if one can't give you all you need.
then why can't we have both.

The things I must have
the things I have already had
are becoming overlapping.
stopping the other from happening.

Theirs

There it lays
Don't touch it
Don't even think of it
Stop I said just look away
Don't let it control you.
Like it has controlled me,
I have had to learn to live,
With it and it is not easy.

There it stays,
Knowing it isn't easier
to walk through the day
and sleep at night.
To hold the ones, you love.
and then turns to evil
with eyes that can reach heaven.

Now you know why I walked the way I do,
how I have become so sick,
but I love you
need you to turn your wants
into tears that everyone can feel.
Their needs firsts.

67 Miles

There is 67 miles,
between your house and mine.
in your heart that is where I linger.
All that driving,
so much time.
you know she knows
how you want me
and I want her.

Stream

We walk the same path
crossing the opposite directions
now we walk together
talk together

I have found a friend
I trust.
You can learn from him
where you can teach me

I have found a friend
whom speaks with the mind
whom loves with the heart
whom knows how to say goodbye
when the time comes
I know how to glance across a room
to make me feel warm
with fire traveling
through my veins
into my blood stream
I found a friend in all of you and me.

Jealousy

Her personality of a child is restraining to all
I feel why you screwed up the lies
walking out on her.
She feels you are in the wrong,
if you would have known then
you might have not slept in her sheets.
With you she would have realized.
She wasn't the one you wanted.
She does not love herself.
She just gives her flesh away to many
as a lie of self-esteem.
Did you ever know her in the time?
Like I have known you?
Did she ever know what you're about?
She jokes about your talent
like it is a game.
Not knowing how it makes you feel
when you take control of the music,
all the ears around you hear it.
Yes,
I know she will never have what I feel.
Yes,
I believe you love me even though
she wanted to put jealousy in my mind to hurt you.
I believe you will only leave me
if the time has to be,

otherwise I am the one
she wants to be.
True, it comes to this.
Truth is what we must speak.

Every Sigh

A smile, a ray
will brighten your day
words from you
could only cure
a soul that is shattered.
From a world that is just sadder
among my cries you hear
Every Sigh, every tear.

Standing from Behind

Why must tears fall
for one to see the pain they caused?
Why must the sadness show through
before happiness can be
Along the way we lost the love
the proof of not losing us.

I believe we can
standing from behind
I see a man,
a boy who is afraid of a dream.
I'm a small girl
in love with a man
who cannot love me,
but I might give love to him.

Deep

deep in my heart
there is a beat
it burns with heat
melts when it weeps

deep in my mind
there is a vision
with many decisions
how to spend as companions

deep in my soul
there is a feeling
that with my thinking
I'm going to have dealings

dealing with those deep unknown feelings

Been Gone

We made it here,
you and I
we have learned
and we have needed.
The time and patience
of others to lend a hand.
The true friends that I had
to call a thousand times
over and over again.
We still have each other
though others have been gone.
The memories we have made
throughout our song.

Have You Become

Tomorrow will bring a day of journeys
I am going back the direction I came.
In a way of knowing paths,
that I would like to travel.
I took to the world
one stop away
to see how I felt with those words
of me.
Only my heart hears
who will smile
to see me
who will need my touch.
Who do you want when everyone is away?
Who do you miss when alone?
It is how you become the direction I come.

Regrets

How many times
have you said, "Never"?
Minutes later you wished
you were so clever.
Regrets are dreams you
wished you had lived differently.
Laughter is reality you could not
have not done a second chance so perfectly.
if given a second chance.
Love is an illusion with
a little different dreaming.
Live, laugh and enjoy all.
with no direction of regretting.

Peace

to

Love

and

Heal

Try

Your voice touches my inner thoughts,
with whispers of sweet kisses and hugs.
I will love your body,
mind, thoughts and mistakes.
Make me laugh and you have got my love forever.
Find my heart and remain mine.
Rub one thought and kiss the other.
Love me and I will make our fantasy come true.

When We Met

I sit here looking out my window,
watching the rain fall.
Just thinking how long,
will our love last.
I do not think I will ever,
be able to say goodbye,
I need you.
When we met, I was so happy.
You taught me to open my eyes again.
If you are here my heart is full,
the day you say goodbye,
part of my heart will be gone too.

Forgetting

It started out as a crush,
and turned into something more.
The love I feel for you,
I have never felt before.
You make me feel so happy,
whenever I am down.
I am glad I can trust you,
whenever you are around.
You are the only one I have wanted,
I want you to know.
No matter what happens,
I will never let you go.

I will never say goodbye,
I want you to stay.
I don't want to forget your face,
hair, eyes, smile, but I am afraid.

What if we never meet again.
If you leave now,
there is one thing I must,
say before you go.
I will always love you,
from the bottom to the top of my heart.

T stands for true,
being trusting to one another,
to listen,
and care,
also be a friend.

L stand for love,
being considerate to one another,
to lend a hand,
and smile,
also know that one.

Love

Love comes in all different ways.
Every place you go there is love.
So, once the love finds you,
or you find it.
Do not let anything come between you
and the one you love.

Look

Love is all in the eyes,
all in the way you looked at me,
all in the way I looked at you.

Then someday,
the way we look at each other,
will bring us closer together.

Love is just a look,
from one's eyes.

Special Night

The sky is clear
the moon is bright
Here we both stand
this beautiful night
The stars sparkle
the trees whistle

We know we love each other
We both feel
each other's tender touch
We pull each other close
Hold on tight
Our lips come together
Touch so very light
I will never forget
This special night

Never Say Goodbye

I finally got you, took a long time.
All those weeks of daydreaming.
All the days spent looking at you.
All the hours I thought of you.
We have had a lot of great memories
and had some bad ones too.
You were there for me
I will always be there for you.
I will stay no matter how rough it gets
I will come out fighting for you,
cause in the end I hope we are together.

Two heart will remain as one

Just You and Me

I look at your picture next to my bed.
Then a smile appears out of the blue,
I wonder without love like yours
what would I do?
You make my frowns into smiles
you brighten every day when your near.
Your kindness makes me want to say, "I love you"
Only when your gone should fall a tear,
washes away the memory.
You come and go as you please
not knowing where you are
or where you have been.
I think every day, why me
I only want to be with you.
Do you feel the same?
I don't know how many times you have hurt me.
You don't slap me,
you don't scream at me,
you just take your love away.
That hurts the most
the day we met I fell in love with you
time or people will never change that.
One day when you're lonely or have the blues,
have got you down,
and love isn't in the air.

I will be there, a friend who cares.
You might change,
I might change
but love goes on forever.

Just for You

Your smile is like the sun rise in the morning.
Your eyes are like the moon,
that shines at night.
Guys have come and gone,
but I want you to know.
I really care for you,
loving you for years.
Never knew how to tell you,
always was afraid you would say goodbye.
Before you knew how I felt.
Wondering if you would feel the same for me?

I want to hold your hand,
walk in the sand.
I want you to hold me
when things have gone bad,
make me happy not sad.
I want to kiss you as the waves roll in,
my heart has been crushed.
My feelings have been hurt,
will you take my heart and emotions?
Hold them tight never letting them go.
I want to be with you forever,
but I know that can't be, at this time being
I want it to be just you and me.

Now and Then

As I look out my window, I see raindrops falling.
All I want to do is dance in the rain.
I hear cracks and booms from the storm,
which keep me in.
The rumbles and shaking of the house,
making me feel all alone.
You are just too far away at this time.

Come rescue me,
take me as far away as can be.
To a place unknown,
where unicorns prance,
mermaids swim.
Maybe a deserted island
with no one around.
Where raindrops fall as crystals,
touching the ground so very gentle.
The only sound around is birds singing,
the trees blowing in the winds.
Where we will dance
to the light of the moon.
You will take me in your arms
promising never to let me go.
With a touch of your lips,
a sound from your voice,
I know our souls are together forever.

The storm is still all around me,
but I just recall.
Every time a storm appears,
I am thinking of the deserted island,
where nothing can go wrong,
in the now and then.

Love is What You Make of It

Love is not just a word,
it can be happy or even sad.
You don't say it unless meant by the heart.
It is a feeling between two people,
that must be so strong,
they know it is love,
and meant to be.
Four letters are all that is needed,
to write it.
To express,
that is a whole different feeling.
If it is there you will see it
even if mistakes happen.
That is what loves about
one thing to remember.
You fall in love;
love is what you make of it.

Eternity

You are all I need.
Is what you said.
An open door to my heart,
you entered on your own.
Tearing down the walls of sorrow.
Now I'm starting all over new
rebuilding love with you.

My life was a tear drop,
now it is a smile.
Dream and wishes of what will be
the future is only time,
that will be spent together or apart.
It's up to us, how things will be,
we choose the roads to our hearts.
That bring our souls together,
eternity is what we need.
We share our love,
we will live together,
love together.

Slowly Apart

Your love is as sweet as our tears
that roll down our face,
when we are sad.
Then we turn and walk away,
why have we changed so much?

We still want each other,
but ashamed of how we both hurt.
We can't go back.

I want what we had,
the way we made each other feel.
You only brought out the good things in me,
and threw away the bad

Now as friends it hurts seeing you
walk hand in hand
with someone else.
Is our love really gone?

`

Have we lost it, just to be found?
We treat each other great,
but we can't touch our hearts.
The way we did before.

We used to share everything,
now we slowly drift apart.
I don't want to lose our love,
but things have got to change.
Time to heal from what we have learned.

Silent Hand

The silent hands that brings us love and strength.
Hold the heavens from the sea of dark.
Where demons rule and demons walk.
Keep them away from the angels of hearts
and truly be honest.

Hex,
the witch with the wand
the one we loved so much.
She changed her ways
now that we live untouched
Carried away to live or die
on our way to the time that is to come.

The way it was done, she had power over love.
Her mind and heart were not bond together.

Only her spells of hatred were though as one.
The world is almost gone,
to her she will be the only one.
Deprivation of her own soul.
Between dust and dawn,
the blindness caught up to her.
Now nothing remains the same.
with the silent hands
that brings us love and strength.

The Long Journey

From boundaries beyond my sight,
I journey to find our love.
The wind blows by me like,
the clouds that roll above.
I reach out to grab what I see
only to find it is a faded memory.

If you should disappear
before my love reaches you.
You should know,
I am hurting and suffering
a long journey alone.

One kiss will make our love true,
one wrong word will make it
sad and blue.
Send a kiss in the wind,
it shall find me.
Say sweet words and they will blow
like rhythms of melody.

Tied Up

Tied up feelings
that is all love is.
In my mind
it starts scattering
I feel great, I feel like smiling.

Press your hand
against the palm of mine
feel the energy of love
transmitting through.
No words spoken,
just one feeling after another.
How could love happen this fast?
It is greatest experience,
you and I holding on to one another
for love and life.
Our hearts are burning with flames.
nothing could dampen our fires.
In this moment I am tied up
with the scattering energy of us.

Another Day Without You

My love for you is pure,
as a newborn,
out of the womb.
I dream you hold me one more day.
We cannot deny our love,
I wish you loved me in
just one more way.
You can't stop the kiss,
after our lips have touched.
We are too close to back away.
Life changes with one word,
bells ring in the clouds above.
If a bird song could be heard,
they'd sing of first loves.
You fill my hunger with your arms
wrapped around me tight.
Never sad,
never lost,
we love together forever to be.
Until the sun goes down
and rises the next morning over the sea.
I gaze upon the doorway
to your soul,
not afraid to enter.
Another day without you,
to grow more for when
we do spend those days together.

Voice

to

Motivate and Speak

reams

Dreams are Dreams
Reality is Reality
all you need is faith,
love and courage.
Then some day
reality will be all a dream.

Dream World

Dream World lets you dream
The most important dreams
Everyone enters the dream world
Only dreams come true
In the dream world
Every time I enter
I will dream of you.

A Child's Dream

A child's dream can be anything
You know they will try their hardest
to make it come true
don't get in the way
of a child's dream
it is the worst thing you can do.

Friend

The faith and trust
a child has for a friend
is much more than someone
there for them
they have love
Peace
and hope in their friend
who will stay a lifetime with them.

Rose Tears

a seed blows from miles and miles away
planting itself in a grain of sand
its life begins in just one day
before you know it, it's out of hand

roots grow under the ground below
stems get tall and very strong
petals sung
wind blew
making a soft sound
everyone knew
never heard before but in a song

tears of heavens fall
songs cannot be heard
for it's not sad
only happiness is what I saw
for when the sky was clear
covered with birds
my love wasn't there to hold me
from the heavens came tears

Hold on to Fate

Problems today, will soon pass
hold on to dreams we have
don't lose the love within,
time will go by too fast.

Love only one,
for they will love you back
think and dream of good times
that had been
and plenty more to come.

One night alone,
can cure a broken heart
soft words
can mend a day of sorrows.

Talk with me, love me.
forgive and understand me,
when I have done wrong.
I will ask of you no more.

I believe in you and trust you
do you feel the same?
I never want to lose you,
Lose us.

Take me in your arms forever,
promise me, and I will promise you.
I am here for your needs
fate will take us where we need to be.

Changing

Same roads every night
Same roads every day.
One more drive around this town
I'm going to go insane.

One more minute
another thought of you
sometimes I hurt,
more days than others.
Love me please, I do.
one more hour,
maybe more day you will come.
in a dream or two.

Time to walk another path
to drive a different road
to give another chance
to change the way
of the forbidden code.

Children

Playing tricks with the mind
No wonder everyone so confused
If a child's mind is fragile
Then these adults need to learn
They have manipulated the mind
That the children do not have
They are what we teach them
harsh lies you tell will destroy their thoughts.
I do not like the deceiving
Making them think they is all they show
For more lies they then we know
More lies then the love
of the women cares to know
They need to calm
a tone in their voice
when children want to play
children want to grow
They need to learn
Sit and teach them well
Their mind is ready
You just cannot turn away
Walk a road to the sun
Until you find the patients you are
You must hold to bear a child of kindness
in the pores of her heart
In the pores of his.

Knowing, for They Spoke

For they spoke of me
not knowing who I was
they spoke good things
that came from your mouth
it felt good when they accepted
knowing who I was sitting here

I feel as if I was reborn this morning
as if all had been lifted
even though your sorrow still ran through
now I am growing to learn you

For they spoke of me
not knowing who I was
they spoke good things
that came from your mouth
I feel good knowing I know you
you know me
when we speak

Notice in My Writings

Notice in my writings that the mind speaks
for if we weren't taught
what we like, we won't love
what to say, you won't speak
what to do, we won't act
what to think, we won't learn
how to be
we would all be someone else.

Notice in my writings that the heart sees
in the existing the heart beats
how the blood runs through
how the heart feels when veins bleed
how the mind goes unnoticed
when the heart thinks
how a manipulating mind works
when the heart knows
how the heart learns
not to trust love.

Notice in my writings that the soul feels
upon the mist of the air
did you feel the chill of breeze go by
upon the mist of the wind
did you hear cues that echoes a room
upon the mist of the ground
did you notice the beat under your feet

upon the mist of the skies
did you see the moon disappear
upon the mist of the body
did you but care when the heart stopped beating.

Notice in my writings that the body is just flesh
and how I beg to hold the hand
that keeps all your promises.
how I beg to walk in the feet
that travel the earth
how I beg to hear through your ears
that way I can hear what you do
how I beg to have your eyes to see beauty
the way you do because I love you.

The Darkest

The darkest sky always has light
to guide the lost
save the young
bare the romance
mourn the sad
wipe the tears
clam the rage
heal the cracks
brighten the land
to see.

The darkest heart always loves
to make one think
save the old
bare forgiveness
fix the broken
sew the threads
soothe the soul
mend the veins
and love the heart
to think.

The darkest mind always has direction
to have them move.
save time
bare travelers
go to the wanders

giving them maps
point the way
drawn in stone
and light the direction
to travel

We all have traveled into the dark.
to only return.

Guardian

I guess this means I am your guardian,
to be here with motherly care.
I love you and
I am not going anywhere,
do not give up hope.
This is just a stepping stone,
for us to conquer.
Once it is completed,
we will not have to look back.
I am not here for a while,
I am here for life
So, get used to it.
I am here to walk with you
throughout the days
and keep you safe at night.
Our journey has just begun,
neither one of us turn away.
So why start now, you are me and
I am you,
it is not easy to split us up.
It will take much,
much more to resist the guardian in me.

Time Moves Before

I sit here in this room of so many
just thinking to myself
how many of these
flesh of veins are lost?
How many have been found?
How many minds do not want to live?
And How many never want to die?
For me I just want to be with you,
even if we died tomorrow.
It would be forever that we had
the love of each other.
We know in this earth of unfamiliar faces.
We found one another for the time now.
Though my one concern is being alone
I do not think life would be life if all
I had was the sand we shared
If death arouse over me, how would you live
Considering I am your angel that protects you
The bond that will not brake
With the moments her eyes await you.
If I ever must leave, I would like
to see her son in her arms
I would like to see her face in joy.
If the angel must take her, to free her of pain
She will miss you
If you do not go home

before her time on earth is done.
She must learn in her prayers
That the only child she gave a life to
Took what she gave and gave life
to others around him
He brought smiles to every face
Never spoke bad words to those
In the course of friends, nameless they all know him
She needs to know he is alive
Before she stops her fight
Pray to God, just please give us
long enough to see her eyes
For the first time he hugs the warmth again in years
Tears wiped away from the eyes that run from joy.

The Grass Grows

In the grass, where the ground is wet
the ants have homes
the sand is hard to find.
You lie me down to see the stars
then and only then
does one fall from the sky.
As it looks like it is becoming closer
you shelter me from the rays,
so I don't burn.
The grass grows over us,
how long have we been here,
we now wake.

It has been years,
only now I have realized,
I am not lost.
I am here to find my mate
who will come with me over valleys
of land far and wide.
Grow with me, young and old.
From a child he will shine on the earth with me.
That is the day when the grass is under our feet,
a path is made we will walk far as one,
but never look back.
We have made our decisions,
so we would end up here.
Now up to us, to go far
God has done his part.

I Am the Land

The woods, the grass, the nature is calling
yes, I would like to walk in it
to the bridge to watch traffic
to the highest point that's near.
The wind,
the mist,
It is catching me in the breeze
The bugs have come out too,
but I must ignore.
For my blood is sweet,
way down deep.
This bridge is high,
my very last memory.
The water
The air
The fire
but I am the land.

Too Sad

In time of need,
I get us.
In time of patience,
I get bothered.
In time of night,
we watch the stars.
In time of day,
we watch clouds drift.
In time of love,
I need to know, do you?
In time of hate,
I need to know, will you?
In time of conversations,
I need to know will you.
Will you love me,
will you hate me,
will you speak
when making up?

Speaking Back

I need to talk,
to tell someone
what is in my head.
Why the voice speaks
to ask if that is my heart.
If my soul is speaking up
for my thoughts go by so fast.
Overwhelmed I forget
to step back and see.
If that is what I want
the reality hits
I stand lost.
Without anyone
to speak to,
still need a mind
with my intelligence
to speak back.

One Good One

No matter what I say
tease you about
the most important thing is
I love you.
More than anything
I just need you
to grow up to be a man
that I need.
Not something I want
but need
I cannot imagine trading you in,
for any other souls.
Flesh of many after you,
someone has or want to give.

I stay the way I am
I know you are me
I desperately need you to be my man
from now in time to death.

You are the only man I could speak to
about any subject
that our nighttime thoughts have to speak.
We are each other
we make one
one good first love.

Words Don't Explain

Days have passed
now I have words to write.
The feeling is still unexplained,
as if words like I love you would be
to unknown and common.
As if me liking you
would make you understand.
Though all I feel
are the most unexplainable feelings
of questions of writing of not knowing.
Not knowing how to say words that have meaning,
are there words that are for the perfect setting?
If only the dreams of my thoughts
could ever be explained by words.
Emotions will draw a picture that the eyes could feel
without words to explain by the book of Webster.

Dear Friend

I lie wrapped in cotton sheets
with a dear friend beside me.
We fill the holes with silent words
fill the cracks with sentences
of encouragement.
The sweet things we speak
a friend very dear to me just to laugh,
talk with bubbles of sheets
and words we sometimes share.
I lie wrapped in cotton sheets
with a dear friend beside me.
We fill the holes with silent words
fill the cracks with sentence
of encouragement.
I think if we, were we,
would we tell us what I want to hear?

Intuition

to

See and to be Aware

The Walk

Tonight,
I walked down a silent,
still almost too calm road.
Coming up on a house,
I glanced in the direction I see,
the arguing of two,
I took a second to ask why.

Sounds never rang out of faces,
that cried a misery in pain.
Watching them,
the sorrow within began to build.
Sadness seemed less important,
among the rain
Walking down the road,
still very much the same.
I saw the shadow of a crying man,
whispering softly under his breath,
I have lost all I had.

What do I do?

My eyes followed his body,
as it fell to the ground.
Watching him the sorrow,
within I began to build wall,
then my tears seemed less revealed,

among the rain.
Continuing down that road,
dawn almost on time,
arriving at the house,
I lay my head to sleep.
I thought of the two arguing,
the man in the road.
How things always seem to repeat,
watching myself in sorrow,
I than began to rebuild.
Wavering through the rain.

That Woman

That woman speaks in a tone of controlling anger
Unanswered she never seems to let go
She speaks with knowledge
Yet she knows nothing

People who work in these walls
Give off a sense of tension
For they have not learned a quiet peace
They have not discovered how
to control their temper
As they think harsh thoughts

Acting as the devil ran through them
sitting among a role wrote in a book
No one has read
No one can find
Yet you and I have left the pages long ago
knowing how to write a book without them
That woman who could not quiet herself
Our love of peace will shine through
Keep sending out that light you and I are.

When You

Now I know what you see
when you look at me
Wonder how you find
the best in me to love
For the pain that lies within
you gaze at me on the beach
You feel as if you felt
or looked at me before
I melted in the sand
you felt I can still there.
My eyes fell behind you
you feel me watching us.
You think I did not see
that I stand above you looking down
You assume you are alone
when you feel the presence of me.

Yes, I am here, when we grow.
Yes, I am near, when far.
Yes, I am shy, when touched.
Yes, I am happy, when pain rises.

 A Dream

There you are, carrying me,
my love, my soul, a dream
give me strength to walk to you.
I was strong, I will go
if the night is not far from you
a dream, was you and I together
were our souls ever one?
The dream had an end
it was a fuzzy one.
It had gotten farther harder
and it is too hard to see.
when it is just a dream.

$\mathfrak{Fancy}$

I enjoy walking with you
in front of many strange faces
I whisper words
hoping you understand
I laugh with tears
when we conversate among ourselves
your smile seems so innocent
and quite fancy.

Why a Tear Falls

Never have I felt complete
even now
something is missing.
I feel the love
I have returned to you.
I feel the flesh
I lay in bed with you.
There is this need
I can't fully understand
I feel so real.
Tears flow
so incomplete
there is a piece never found
When my soul and mind
wonder together,
if only I knew the need that
so very few know.
When those few have
other thoughts
then of me
so little I feel the pain.
When I do it hurts,
where are the ones?
Who understands?

I can just imagine
they are somewhere
they must be
not understanding
why I have a tear.

Said

Don't speak
your thoughts are safe with me
I know your thoughts
before you say a reason
of a thousand words
you must not need
your heart will beat
when your body laid in bed
where you rest your head
your thoughts patiently rise
from your mind
somewhere from behind
I found
your thoughts
that had been said
they are that way
at night when you
rest your head.

We Dreamed

The world use to go by so fast
we dreamed
we needed
begged and pleaded
to be the speed of the world
when now the time has gone
the pain nears
the dreams fall
eyes learn to weep
I thought I could look at you
I thought you could look at me
did you but not see
what my eyes always saw

My journey began alone
now it is going where I have brought it
I ran into a little bad weather
after the rain
after the storms
have gone
when all is calm
I merely became one
one with the journey
I began
the one I began alone

Leo Heart

You made me feel as a Leo heart always does.
I have loved female and male.
Though the touch was different
that mind always had something to say
without a word
just my touching my soul.

The overwhelming smile gazed on my face
after kissing you goodbye
one I will surely see you again.

If we met in a garden or over my bed of lace leaves
where I would gaze at you from a distance
your beauty from the glass in your eyes
is where I see you.

A friend I hope always
maybe a lover
in time of passing we grow.

A place in my heart the giggle I hear
innocence behind those eyes
is where I want to travel with you.

Will you walk with me?

Before the End

A love that is always remaining
A friend of a thousand stones
That I will fall from a smile apart
Of a life that is yours
A small gift that brings you to me

We grow,
We play,
We know,
We say,
Those little words that hurt
Those little words that is certain
To end our journey

The eyes that hide a man
I know soon he will see in that women
His needs will be felt
His wants will be heard
the echoes of her man's fears.

The journey of the path connecting to others
Ends with the road of mother
The tear must fall for one to give
A hand must reach
before one can comfort the man.
Who knows his heart, before the start.

Absorb

I felt the body of hate
I would rather feel my body ache.
With everyday becoming another
the place I would like to be is here with you.

The music fills the room high
the lights shine and brighten our eyes.
The couch becomes our place to absorb us
through every sense in the flesh of you and me.

To Live

Do you wonder if people
look at you the way you look at them?
What if they really think,
if it compares to what they say?
How many lies must be told before one gives up?
Who do you trust?
Who do you believe in?
How do people change overnight?
What is love if trust never told a lie?
What is love if one can't see past the skin?
Deep in the eyes there is a soul
with no lies just one person.
With another to love everything
that their soul must give.
The one who will love me,
will never be able to live without us.
Their nights would be lonely,
their days will be without feelings.
Without me by their side,
I would be the only true feeling
that their heart and soul would need to live.

Rest My Head On

Trapped in time is how I feel;
there is so much I have.
So much to give,
very few know how a soul feels
when two people have it
at love.
A kiss will tell a thousand truths,
about a soul that feels the flesh.
A glance will tell a million lies,
It will all be forgotten,
if two people can learn to be honest.

Love with us,
no lies,
no battles,
no competition
for the love of another.

My soul alone with few,
they come,
they go,
they leave,
at the end.

The one that will complete me,
will know me before I love him.
He will brighten my eyes

show me the world.
He will take my body to places
I have never been before.
My soul will seep through my pores
into the sand of the earth
that he rests my head upon.

Calming

I see my eyes,
my smile,
my voice
echoing back.
Why do I?
How can I find home?
Walk with me
the stories of my soul
you have rushing out of your beauty
shows the deer out
and calms your purrs.

New to You and Me

Now that I rest my head in a new place
I feel the weather has changed for good grace
Those who I have wrote love and feelings for
Somewhere turned the needs of more
Far from my curious mind
through the one I need to find.
The trust to love within,
the want to be my friend.

When many years of past
There will be only a hand full to last
Next to your side we see many faces
Of the many you seek in different places
Which ones understand when you weep.
Which one holds you through the heap
One will live within the trust
to remove the rust.

She is the one
and he is the song
She had been
looking for all along.

Looking So

Why do you look so mysterious to me?
You hide behind your eyes
with thousands of ideas.
Thoughts that could lead in so many directions
with a mind that travels in what you say.
For people should listen when you talk.
For what you speak seems so real
where your mind is
happens to be so pleasant
to the one of the person
who spoke or knew.
What you thought before
You happened to speak
You hold a lot
I feel there are things I see
I know in you I see
Things not many know
It seems to me

Why must I crave to know
what lurks in your head
as your mind changes so rapidly.
I watch as your eyes journey
from one project to another
as you lay peacefully.
It seems so real to me.

Which Is Me?

When time is over
I am looking back
time is so empty
nothing I could find
just a life of dreams.
Sharing with someone
was a dream I had
I wanted a desire
for that love of all
a journey of dreams.

Not to just want me
not to just need me
just to be me, loved
see me as a soul
between us, was me.

Resilience

to

Know and to Learn

Journey to Growth

I look at the many older faces,
being that I am 21,
it seems like eternity.
How did they make it so far
with life being so fragile?
In one second a life could be undone.
For every step and heartbeat
were in the right direction.
Too many more years
to get where they are.
The journey that I must go on
to see what they saw.

Willing to Learn

Sometimes I fall apart,
when I want to touch.
Sometimes when we touch,
I feel like a drifting soul.
Sometimes I look at you
and need to know,
where you are inside.
I hold your hand,
the hand of one with no soul,
You kneel beside my bed,
to kiss me goodnight.
A warmth over the skin,
I feel the soul drift into you.
Through your eyes you look at me.
I see the one I could love.
I want you to be my inspiration in life.
I want you to help me grow.
I am writing to learn
if you have time to teach.

Don't

Don't speak
If hurt is from
the voice you leak
Don't stay
If there is more
For you away.
Too many times
I have envied a body
Too many times
I have wanted a friend
Too many times
I have wanted to cry
Over the loss of another
Each time I grow
we grew apart
For every lesson I learn
there is one I have lost
The next step is tomorrow
yesterday I have learned
what years of pain I have endured.
Don't cry,
unless this is finally goodbye.
Don't wait to move on to the truth of you.

Her

What was it about me
that made you journey my way
when I sat in that chair facing you.
What made your smile shine on me
inside me your voice filled a craving
that I yearned for.
All my pain seemed to dry up
as you fulfilled the need I wanted
for every moment.
It made me desire more to know you
to know if you were a true soul
inside the beautiful flesh
with perfection of her.

Growth

I'm the one who dreams,
dreams that turn into reality.
I'm the one who has fairytales
that don't come true.
I'm the one who will fall in love
with that someone
who can never quite give me all I need.

If love was like a book
then it would always end.
If love was a poem
it would be every feeling inside of you.

I believe love is a growth that people need
to show that one can find another.
Love can find them in any direction
and then it will never end.
A soul can't unbound from what it becomes.

Understanding Love

In years they will find the real soul.
It creeps
It seeps
It melts its way through the skin,
to the other soul that comprehends

The soul that transfer two into one
That split for a day
Connect at night
and can read a mind
before the other has spoken a word.

I am up here for the eyes to see
you are down there looking up to me.
I need a hand to feel this feeling
for one strong enough
to ease my pain into healing.

Gathering Souls

Quietness fills the room,
people of many gatherings,
Gather-in-one
one excited by another one.

As the room filled with silence
you could faintly hear two souls conversating
and finding one another at last.

Does it matter if they love or hate
the one that is home with the one their meeting.
The first embrace running thoughts
in their head all day,
as if I couldn't see the eyes of lies.

One must place the words in there
through their ears for them to cherish.
Those who fear to see behind their hidden secrets.

Changing Thoughts

A thought can race through a mind 100 times
a day never to be the same,
but as you held her and told secrets of yours.
She would listen
that memory would remain the same
that is where I failed.
I could never listen long enough,
but I can feel your fear.

I'm Sorry...

If one should ever trust again, should I
You prove to my heart
Yours has no certain beat
Except for the feelings you had at a moment in time.
When you place your memories away to hide.

I will be your best friend,
a great lover of lifetimes.
Will I ever be what those few too many might
be in the minutes or hours of your time.
The clock has stopped time for truth.
I don't care how hard it hits.
I want to stop the pain now
before the chase of goodbye is forgotten.
When you are in a minute or an hour,
of your life that I can't fulfill.

Being There

I want to be in your mind and thoughts
across the room I can explain in words
you have never felt
and never stopped long enough to care
for anyone.

When souls lie in this unexplainable fluid
that flows through every part of that body.
Your pores are too deep to flow out
the fluids from your soul.
It will guide you to the others,
for you to later find.
The more we love, the harder the pain comes,
from all the lessons learned.
I dream of fairies
floating into your soul
connecting to you and me.

Falling

Falling down the tunnel,
pictures becoming clear to me.
Lost in time my flesh so far from my body
one gleam of light then dark again.

Falling down the tunnel,
towards a spinning light I fall.
I see feet of a dark man upon the wooden floors
then his toes wiggle and he is gone,
dark again, blackens.

Falling down the tunnel,
towards a spinning a light I crash.
I witness kitchen cabinet's swing their doors
then they melted, ripped and torn, falling.

Ripped Away

I remember a small child
sitting at a table coloring.
She looked at me while I faded away.
Where does the light begin?
Where did it end?

Wish I could have been there,
to lend a hand.
When she was ripped from the air, into hard land.
She stands without a tear,
dreaming of the right man to hold her hands.
Remembering the words, I spoke,
things I needed not broken,
upon that I recall her listening that night.
Seeing her in a loving world of illusions
spending time thinking of this woman to be.
We ran through small conversation
never did she ask for me to leave or be gone.
In my head I recall the look she gave to me
when I said I could not remember
her name after so long.

Deep down I wonder does she notice me?
If we played the part of friends.
Time would tell if we could love
each other's heart in the end.

Quiet Moment Alone

I took a long walk on a path in no direction.
These roads had so many meanings,
yet the thoughts of the world came rushing by
each step gave us a new meaning
of the time I spent alone.
Taking a clock by its arms
we had the strongest to hold,
on the growth of time I needed.
One runs in circles for others
the time spent alone seemed important.
Though I needed that moment
quietly alone.

Set in Stone

Open a door to many faces.
How many will come in?
using the strength and will we have.
In life doors can remain open.
allowing everyone to enter and exit.
In life there are many doors,
that have locks.
Few have keys, maybe that is how they stay.
There are tons of closed doors, no one can enter.
Those are to be our memories
of everyone's life before.
Owners of these doors,
have some trouble entering memories
that they wish they had never lived.
Though they thought they could erase the memory
already set in stone.

Printed in the United States
By Bookmasters